HYPATIA'S WAKE

Also by Susan Andrews Grace

Water Is the First World
Ferry Woman's History of the World
Flesh, A Naked Dress
Love & Tribal Baseball
Philosopher at the Skin Edge of Being

HYPATIA'S WAKE

poetry by

SUSAN ANDREWS GRACE

INANNA poetry & fiction

Toronto, Ontario, Canada
www.inanna.ca

The publisher gratefully acknowledges the support of the Canada Council for the Arts and the Ontario Arts Council. The publisher is also grateful for the financial assistance received from the Government of Canada.

Cover design: Val Fullard

Library and Archives Canada Cataloguing in Publication

Title: Hypatia's wake / poetry by Susan Andrews Grace.
Names: Grace, Susan Andrews, 1949- author.
Series: Inanna poetry & fiction series.
Description: Series statement: Inanna poetry & fiction series
Identifiers: Canadiana (print) 20220243123 | Canadiana (ebook) 20220243182 |
ISBN 9781771339094
(softcover) | ISBN 9781771339100 (HTML) | ISBN 9781771339117 (PDF)
Classification: LCC PS8563.R31 H97 2022 | DDC C811/.54—dc23

Printed and bound in Canada

Inanna Publications and Education Inc.
210 Founders College, York University
4700 Keele Street, Toronto, Ontario M3J 1P3 Canada
Telephone: (416) 736-5356   Fax: (416) 736-5765
Email: inanna.publications@inanna.ca   Website: www.inanna.ca

CONTENTS

A Gloss of Tangled Language Relevant to Invisibility, A Thread of Déréliction

Def. Noun

> 1. Double bind - (psychology) an
> unresolvable dilemma; situation
> in which a person receives
> contradictory messages from a
> person who is very powerful
> 2. A situation in which a person
> must choose between equally
> unsatisfactory alternatives; a
> punishing and inescapable
> dilemma.

> *Syn.* Dilemma, Quandary
> State of uncertainty or perplexity
> especially as requiring a choice
> between equally unfavorable
> options
> (.)(.)

Bind a gloss

> *verb transitive 1.(. To tie or*
> *fasten with a cord* umbilical or
> dressing gown or roman shade
> *2.(. To fasten, encircle, gird* the
> underwear, where we are, under

where we were. *3.(. To bandage up, swathe, often with up* or slathered with love = y = x + extra y chromosome = outside the mathematical suicide the double x chromosome commits as it wants *4.(. To constrain or obligate, as by moral authority* binding the you to the me to = we, first person plural, the philosophical we, lost in its strictures, we are the others, Virginia Woolf's outsiders, forever outside church, university, law the binding of *5.(. Law: to subject to a definite legal obligation* and *6.(. To stitch, fasten together and enclose between covers* under the covers, undercover we sew our eyes and ears and mouths shut to conform to law and *7.(. To provide with a border for reinforcement or decoration* The housewife's soul as big as the house and bigger; as the earth, so below, beyond the narrow good, the cord or tie *8.(. To cause to cohere; cement* her relationship to household fealty, faulty as the foundation on which it is built *9.(. To constipate*, as in history, third leg of the stool *10.(. To make irrevocable; seal* as in a bargain, some bargain *11.(. To apprentice or indenture, often with, out, or over* as household enslaved people, held in arms of domesticity and democracy which can't afford freedoms in creatures meant for pleasure *12.(. To tie up anything* is to have control *13.(. To cohere, stick together* the boys' club or old boy's club *14.(. To have binding force, be obligatory* is what's going on below *15.(. To become stiff and hard as cement, jam or gears* (to say nothing of jammed gears or he good-naturedly gave her the gears.) *16.(. Music, to tie* Musical phrase to be tied over to one's lover is to understand how binding—**in a bind** can be. *US Informal* Or formal, for that matter, what matters in a tight situation. [OE *bindan*] doubly. (.)(.)

Double, a gloss
adjective

1.(. Combined with another usually identical one: repeated: a double consonant, double vibration, voiced or voiceless, made by contact or constrictions, click clack, click clack, stiletto music, chains, her life in chains *2.(. Two together; two combined: double lines* or lives: double day not a publisher but a diurnal reality *3.(. Having two parts, applications, function,* functions etc. two-fold, duple *4.(. More than one; not single; dual:* a *double* role *5.(. Consisting of two layers* laid end to end across the earth *6.(. Made for two:* a *double* bed across the earth, things made for two *7.(. Twice as great, as large, as many etc.,* a *double* fare, a *double* day, a *double* load but unfair *8.(. Extra heavy, large, wide etc.:* a *double* blanket, double-woven, thick, pulled to his side even though he's the warm one *9.(. Marked by duplicity; two-faced:* a *double* life, street angel, home devil, Mr. Jones *10.(. Music producing tones one octave lower than the notes indicated on a score: said of an instrument* of *11.(. Botany, Having the petals increased in number* lotus flower, for example

Double

noun

1.(. Something that is twice as much as *2.(. One who or that which closely resembles another; duplicate* Oh we do resemble each other in our complicity; we think this is normal *3.(. A player or singer who can substitute for another, understudy for domesticity,* there is always another ready to take her place, whoever she is, never irreplaceable because she is Aristotle's flowerpot, waiting to be planted with seed. The beer-gutted, middle-aged man rarely at a loss for company, a mystery which may become sacred, someday soon a pope will declare it one of the joyful, sorrowful, glorious or luminous mysteries in the Church of Man *4.(. In motion pictures, one who substitutes for a star in dangerous feats* We do that, stand in for a Marilyn or a Meryl or a Mae West, in the dangerous feats of love and marriage and babies and riveting rivets, dividing divots, the dust of which we are made 5.(. *A sharp or backward turn, as of a hunted fox* The hunts aren't over. They continue, gods and dogs and bitches alike hunting the bushy-tailed vixen 6.(. *A trick or stratagem* Hunters tell us they are not tricks, just accidents of history or idiots or the combination thereof 7.(. *A fold or pleat.* Folding the laundry, the pastoral fold, the sheep fold deeply resonate, the kick pleat a kicker in the behind of a skirt's temptation but allows the woman to walk away, in church as elsewhere 8.(. *Eccl. A feast at which the antiphon is said both before and after the psalms.*

Amen. The song that keeps repeating, double time, double life a responsive versicle, *doublet of anthem 9.(. Pl. In tennis, etc., a game having two players on each side,* like keeping up with the Joneses, the couple scene 10.(. *In baseball, a fair hit that enables the batter to reach second base without benefit of an error.* But the question is, what is a fair hit. Mr. Jones hasn't stopped hitting. He reached second base on the fourth date, a long time ago. Without the benefit of an error on his wife's part she's now just batty *11.(. In bridge, the act of challenging an opponent's bid by increasing its value and thus the penalty if the contract is not fulfilled; also, a hand warranting such an act*

(.)(.)

On the double
Double time
Quickly,
doubling

Double

verb transitive

*1.(. To make twice as great in
number, size, value, force, etc.* as
in making the patriarchal family
grow *2.(. To be twice the
quantity or number of* women as
needed to improve the quality of
offspring *3.(. To fold or bend
one part of upon another; make
of two thicknesses: usually* with
over, up, back. As in bending
over backwards to do the right
thing by the family, often, to
experience that feeling of being
bent *4.(. To clench* (the fist):
often with *up* one side and down
another side of the fair sex *5.(.
Naut. To sail around: to double
a cape*, under which is a heart,

11

deemed breakable because it's female south of the border between the land of hier and the land of archy. Sacred orders abound, that's what hierarchies do, order everyone they can *6.(. Music, To duplicate a voice or part in unison or in another octave,* always in harmony *7.(. In baseball,* oh always in baseball, *to advance (a base runner) by making a two-base hit: he doubled her home.* In the honeymoon phase, of the abuse cycle a double winner *8.(. In bridge to challenge (an opponent) by announcing a double* with the perfect helpmate, intelligent and educated, up to a point.

OF<L *duplus,* double

(.)(.)

DOUBLE BIND THEORY

A dilemma in communication, individual
or group hears two or   more
conflicting messages,
one response   negates the other.

Failure assured, confrontation
impossible. Not a simple, no—
                paradox
like a bad dream

             punishment
inevitable.

Two injunctions necessary   conflict,
do both   *but only if you want to.*

Third injunction,
no escape, no matter what you choose.

The double

     bind

          requires

     An   intense
relationship   in
which to exist,
the   kind   in
which   it   is
imperative   to
act
appropriately.
The   important
person in the
relationship
(not   you,
obviously) will
tell   you
contradictory
things.

     You   are   not
allowed   to
notice   the
confusion and
not allowed to

decide   which
of   the
utterances   to
respond   to
first.
(.)(.)

THE GENEALOGY THREAD

Knot

Intertwining rope, one free end
being passed through a loop
drawn tight, but also

A lump thus made or

Ornamental bow of silk, lace,
braid or other narrow goods or

A hard, gnarled portion of a tree or

Cross-grained mark on lumber
sawn or

Cluster or group of things or

People such as those on the
church steps

After the wedding ceremony,

A bond or union, the marriage
knot

Enlargement in a muscle or

A problem, something not easily
solved

or

In nautical terms, a division of
log time,

        marked by pieces of
        cloth or knotted strings

        at equal distances, and
        used to determine the
        rate of a ship's motion

        which followed the stars
        above and made
        Hypatia invisible.

Hypatia's father Theon was a poet of the starry sky
*and author of "On Signs and the Examination of Birds and
Croaking of Ravens." As a believer in magic, astrology, and divination
he was more the norm in Alexandria than Hypatia whose somewhat
rational attitude to the world was curious and out of place.*

Knot

History swept clean of Hypatia's childhood:

     a day no one recorded.

        Untangle

        Her mother puts the scrolls away, tells young

Hypatia

        to go outside and play.
        Hypatia turns to the bright outdoors, hot
            dust blowing pink on the threshold:
        heat rises as she walks to her swimming practice:
              she's still thinking: *water fills the blood,*
                      grasses the stomach
        she walks like a straw doll
        subject to the sun, great source,
        in the sky every morning,

        begins her travel
        through the cosmos.

LIFE OF HYPATIA

by Socrates Scholasticus from his *Ecclesiastical History*

THERE WAS *a woman at Alexandria named Hypatia, daughter of the philosopher Theon, who made such attainments in literature and science, as to far surpass all the philosophers of her own time. Having succeeded to the school of Plato and Plotinus, she explained the principles of philosophy to her auditors, many of whom came from a distance to receive her instructions. On account of the self-possession and ease of manner, which she had acquired in consequence of the cultivation of her mind, she not unfrequently appeared in public in presence of the magistrates. Neither did she feel abashed in going to an assembly of men. For all men on account of her extraordinary dignity and virtue admired her the more. Yet even she fell victim to the political jealousy which at that time prevailed. For as she had frequent interviews with Orestes, it was calumniously reported among the Christian populace, that it was she who prevented Orestes from being reconciled to the bishop. Some of them, therefore, hurried away by a fierce and bigoted zeal, whose ringleader was a reader named Peter, waylaid her returning home, and dragging her from her carriage, they took her to the church called Caesareum, where they completely stripped her, and then murdered her with tiles.* After tearing her body in pieces, they took her mangled limbs to a place called Cinaron, and there burnt them. This affair brought not the least opprobrium, not only upon Cyril, but also upon the whole Alexandrian church. And surely nothing can be farther from the spirit of Christianity than the allowance of massacres, fights, and transactions of that sort. This happened in the month of March during Lent, in the fourth year of Cyril's episcopate, under the tenth consulate of Honorius, and the sixth of Theodosius.*

Notes

* The Greek word is **ostrakois,** literally "oyster shells," but the word was also applied to brick tiles used on the roofs of houses.

Hypatia was born around 355 CE, in Alexandria—
she didn't spring from Zeus's forehead.

Knot

Philosophy is the one thing they will not allow a woman to do—
                                        writes Luce Irigaray.
My friend Jacqueline tells me that drinking gin while reading
                                        Irigaray helps.

In a khamaseen wind
particles a little larger than light waves
scatter red, cause a blue sun more rare
than the blue moon
but also as Egyptian.
                    Untangle

                    Philosophy not allowed:
                            Alexandria's ancient seaside—
                            history's constancy; conquerors
                            and conquered; humanity and
                            scholarship without a mother.

                    The sea older—
                    she sparkles whether poisoned
                    or not, reflects light as does the lucky stone of Isis,
                    famous lighthouse at sea's edge.

The Woman at Alexandria—Daughter in *Déréliction*

   i
(.)(.)

Sank into air,

       history bracketed a daughter

       gone from literature and science.

       Our consolation: her name

       lost in time's wake, past,

       time to celebrate

Hypatia.

Hypatia was the daughter of Theon
scholar, mathematician, astronomer, and
member of the Museum, or in Greek, ohoek tou mouseiou.

Knot

Silken knots, like motherlessness,
are worst—
untwisted floss tangled
even by breath.

Think—
      fingers in cobwebs
no milk, no silk.

            Untangle

            To spin silk, hands must be
            smooth as rose petals
            or newborn skin.
            Rub with lemon juice and,
            depending upon available humidity,
            sesame milk may be used as hand lotion
            or to soak fibres before handling.

Bombyx mori caterpillars—
after thirty days of eating
mulberry leaves: a silk worm

rotates two hundred thousand times
       in three days
       not dizzy
but weaves a silky cocoon
out of his spinneret—
       a hole in his head—
fibre the length of
       twelve football fields.

ii
(.)(.)

Men came to listen to Hypatia.

No women students, we assume. None noted.

> Money
> has value;
>
> women have worth,
> sometimes.

But why pay for the milk when the cow is free, close the barn door
after the horse has left?

> Silence doesn't cost a penny.

Hypatia had worth, auditors, and her own name—

> sometimes when money's missing,
> women have auditors.

Most women in the fourth century were known by relationship
my woman or *his woman*.

Her mother was probably called
woman, no capital W.

Much to be said for the efficacy of a name
but a price to pay.

Hypatia lived in intellectual and political freedom
until October 15, 412, CE, the day the bishop Theophilus died.
Even though he caused resentment among Alexandrians and
pagans and desert Christians, she and her students had been
safe under his rule as patriarch.

Knot
Orestes visits Hypatia, his command weighty,
her freedom a star in Alexandria's fifth-century sky.
        The giant god Serapis destroyed already by 391 CE,
monks' axes into the god's jaw, his blue skin
composed of gold, silver, lead, tin, and ground
sapphire, hematite, emerald, and topaz crumbled
before the Christian ideal.

                    Untangle
                    Some say Hypatia *is* the library of Alexandria.
                    The city more and more Christian—
                    Africa desolate.

Woman/mother pleasure her sex, silk, pried apart,
Hypatia's body, bleeding torso, dismembered
limbs quiver as the fire consumes her.
A band of monks, her murderers—
        fire mirrors soul, concave,
        reflecting their gaze.

iii
(.)(.)

Alexandria forever is Alexandria *minus* Hypatia.

Think of the day after Hypatia's murder—

> water, universal solvent, rain,
> pools and puddles diluted her blood,
> and sorrow between paving stones.

Solution of condolence *equals* water of equivalency.

> Hypatia's first Alexandria was her mother's womb
> her mother's waters were the great fluidity
> their placenta was negotiation
> woman is watershed plus dividing rivers of water and air.

Woman philosopher *equals* watershed plus no return.

Immediately after her death Hypatia was revered
mostly as a mathematician and her philosophical
stature was diminished by detractors.

Knot

The oxen walk toward Hypatia and me, who swim
in Sigmund's river of consciousness. The oxen seem
to walk on air, stand on top of the fire tower,
sniff the breeze, then hunker and kneel:
   flesh oiled in sacrament, semen tied off,
   ornamental vesicles deep inside
   their fat bodies.

Oxen, mature first tools of agriculture, bovines with an education,
most useful animals in Egypt, in their perfect collaboration
sit upon the height, a jingle of gold and waxed olivewood shudder—

paradox of liberation—

like women who claim body, mind, and soul unto themselves.

     Untangle

     Burden and draught and plough redundant
     as they shelter neutered genius
     nestled between hind legs, oxen not *same*,
     not *other*. Utility,
     on the shore of consciousness,
     holds Hypatia hostage.

iv
(.)(.)

Hypatia held her own with the mighty of Alexandria.

They'd have said in the 1950s,
She thought like a man.

Truth was, men thought like her.

Bind and tangle doubled—
        her self-possession
        a crime, retroactively.

Maybe she squared the circle or saw its folly
fifteen centuries early.

No one knows.

She gave intellectual attention freely,

academic promiscuity—her fault.

Church history sees Cyril, Theophilus's nephew and successor,
as a great theologian and dogmatist but in his own time he was
seen as power-hungry and caused dissent, especially usurping
power of the prefect, Orestes, and persecuting and expulsing Jews.

Knot

Erection of phalli— the gesture that excludes,
cultures built around their tumescence and seasonal deflations.

Quick and easy erections, they last for centuries.

> The forgotten, unthinkable, and un-thought,
> passed over—feminine.

We wait for the gesture that beckons men and women,
severally and equally, into dreams of seeds, sowers, folds,
earth, and we pray not for what we deserve.

> Untangle

> A forgotten mother, we hope, will not notice
> her own absence in the vale of cold and misery
> or that we have not built a home for her.

> That mother has no coins or pocket gods, she is
> abandoned in *déréliction*: a desert in winter:
> our ignorance.

> She cannot trust us enough to reveal
> warm springs underfoot. She stays forgotten.

> What drowns—
>   slits open questions.

The Woman at Alexandria—Daughter in *Déréliction*

v
(.)(.)

Neither did she feel abashed in going to an assembly of men,
wrote Socrates Scholasticus.

Hypatia belonged to no man, hallmark of a virgin.

She possessed full control—
>power and faculties, presence of mind,
>remarkable in celebrity of any era.

>A woman thought, taught men.

She needed self-possession, young men
falling in love with her, all over the place.

Hypatia was respected by city rulers and loved
by her disciples. There is no doubt—every account mentions it.

Knot

Paradoxical, Hypatia's dilemma in Alexandria—
      she goes into the streets as a free woman
      is killed on the way home because
      she goes into the streets as a free woman.

Cyril sees extra chariots parked
outside her house and is jealous.
His god is jealous for Cyril
(in case he doesn't have enough jealousy for himself)
his god is known for that.

A refresher on how jealous gods work
and minds like Cyril's create—
      alterity means woman and man differ
      divinity   means a masculine god needs holy men to represent him
      ethics are conclusions drawn from the above

          young women
          cut to pieces,
          fed to pigs,
          in Vancouver.

                Untangle

                Old commandment in a new ethic
                Thou Shalt Not Kill.

                Face of the other untangles knots
                that killing tightens as it strangles.

vi

(.)(.)

We hardly notice that Socrates Scholasticus
mentions un-abashedness in his short biography.

The double bind triples its pink tangle
in our hair during a sleep of centuries.

Get a whiff of hot sun: truth strikes.

Hypatia ought to have been abashed for not noticing the bind,
she who lived in a Roman colony, among vulgar Romans.

Ligare: Latin verb to bind or tie or connect

Religion—re-*ligare*—re-bind—re-tie—re-connect.

Even though Hypatia was not *of* the religion—she died of it.

The manner of Hypatia's murder was common
in Alexandria, which tended toward anarchy, and thereafter
launched into silence about the event and its perpetrators.

Knot

A twenty-first century Chinese baby girl
born to destitute silk farmers who've moved to the city,
is given up for adoption to North Americans
who consume silk clothing.

                    Untangle

                    Cosmic economy:
                              no thing is of value,
                              measure of alterity
                                        cruel as silk,
                                        kind as a slit throat.

vii
(.)(.)

Political jealousy, mask for fear, reveals perceived inequities,
poisonous heart of Alexandria.

Hypatia asked for it.

Had she been afraid she may not have been murdered.

Her fault was the no-faultness of politics—
      she was not jealous.

She should have been, she should have known.

Conversely, perhaps she did know, saw jealousy,
took a chance.

Hypatia's misfortune—
      she was accustomed to respect
      in spite of the constant *déréliction*
      for women in her culture which meant

               Hypatia lost her mother in her story.

               History lost Hypatia and

               her mother's name—no story.

Socrates Scholasticus reports Christian men spread a rumour that Hypatia
was the lion in the path of reconciliation between the bishop, Cyril, and the prefect, Orestes. "Rumour" is key.

Write Hypatia to understand history
full of dust, the Lord always with her
and the Marys, blessed are they among women
and blessed is the perfect thunder,
her mind, forgotten. Hypatia's ghost survives.

Remember.

Step outside:
        best understanding resides
beyond
        Plato's cave
behind the ideal, we are subjects to
exasperated speleology, a philosophy which
        demands ignorance of the mother's
        name, with exceptions, of course,
        made for the mothers of gods.

::   Man of action who wanted to write but was instead
a reluctant bishop, defender of the weak and helpless, a funny man
who wrote brilliantly about his baldness
and ill-fated journeys by sea, as well as
unrequited letters to Hypatia, his teacher.

::   Rich man, old money, his wealth from traffic of the herb *silphium*,
genus *Ferula*, tonic and oral contraceptive—
we don't have to wonder why *silphium* quickly
became an extinct species.

::   He lived in a paradise of heart-shaped seedpods,
giant fennel on coins of his realm.

::   The heart's curve in Hypatia's mathematical language
         arc

$$\textbf{\textit{cardioid}}$$
$$(x^2 + y^2 - 1)^3 - x^2 y^3 = 0$$

::   Our Valentine's cards came from his contraceptive,
economic stronghold of Cyrene.

::   The Cyrenaica, his family's luscious tableland since antiquity,
one thousand eight hundred feet above the sea,
rich in olives and grapes, the Mediterranean,
clear and chlorophyll-blue, dazzles below.

::   Hypatia's most famous student because his letters to her survive,
he sets history's precedent regarding Hypatia—

Hypatia lectured on ontology
and ethics, mathematics, and astronomy.

We know nothing of Hypatia's maternal ontology.

A situation common in any age—

we know only that her father Theon,
Alexandrian librarian, wanted to
make a perfect human of his daughter.
And that Synesius wrote to her
his letters survived.
And hers didn't.

Feminine imagination and eternal
    knowledge
as her cells dream in exultation.
The great fluidity loves and pares
civilization with timeless devotion.

Synesius to Hypatia, 1

I seemed destined to play the part of an echo. Whatever sounds I catch,
these I repeat. I now pass on to you the praises of the marvelous Alexander...
—written 394 CE

Synesius's seven letters to Hypatia,
plenitude in a vacuum of evidence—
  she existed—addressed her as The Philosopher,
  loved her mind and teachings, loved her friends,
  such as his uncle Alexander, and hated her enemies.

  Bumbly bishop of Ptolemais records his life,
  an echo. We wonder why she didn't write back (or if she did, why
  her letters were mislaid or stolen in the deserts of Libya
  on their way to him)—
                we don't know.

We can't know fluidity of future or past—
  we leave Synesius of Cyrene wanting to hear.

This early letter ends abruptly.

Hypatia rode her chariot through cosmopolitan Alexandria
wearing a philosopher's tribon. The fibre is not mentioned,
probably cotton, linen, or wool—not likely silk.

What happens when sacrifice goes unnoticed—
rose petals fall, trampled, unseen, perfume evaporates,
silk not harvested, unspun, unwoven, and
girl babies killed, more and more, unnoticed but
not by their mothers.

A godly woman, as in semi-divine,
murdered by men of God.

Hypatia defended Christians to the pagans
and vice versa.
She honoured no gods herself
quite brazen of her.

Synesius to Hypatia, 2

I am breathing an air tainted by the decay of dead bodies. I am
waiting to undergo myself the same lot that has befallen so many
others, for how can one keep any hope, the sky is obscured by the
shadow of birds of prey?

—written 401 CE

The soldiers abandoned their posts—
forgot how to protect territory of the Cyrenacae
so accustomed were they to the wages of peace.

Synesius gathered a small army
to save his people and soldiers.

He hasn't told Hypatia.
She would have expected anyone under her sign
to do the same, he informs her,
in the shadow of vultures.

On a day in March, 415, led by Peter, a lector or reader
possibly of lower holy order, the mob of monks killed her.

Four centuries before Hypatia's death, Antony of Alexandria
heard invisible processions, and therefore set a precedent for Cyril.

In Antony's day, Cleopatra was guilty:
    she, temptress/object
    bewitched the statesman Antony,
    ruler of the eastern provinces of Rome.

    Cleopatra masterminded sequential roasting of twelve boars
    in the royal kitchen, says Plutarch, to please and provide
    a boyish holiday for Antony: ancient fast food and much waste:
        a staycation, the kitchen always ready to accommodate his
    hunger, in case
    his hunger is
    now.

One has to wonder how Cleopatra did it. Unlike Hypatia, she was not
    too beautiful: they could never accuse her of that.
    Cleopatra spoke many languages.
    Born of a shallow gene pool, she strangled a husband,
    pleased Caesar by rolling out of a carpet in his living room
    and seduced him forthwith.
    She was the mother of twins, ruler of many lands, and builder
    of one monument, for her dead lover, Julius. Four centuries later
    the Caesareum, with its porticos on the shore, its libraries,
    gardens, and gates   would hold Hypatia's dead body.

Antony never had enough of anything.

Cleopatra accommodated every insufficiency,
travelled to him with gilded stern, purple sail, silver
oars,
and demanded he board her ship,
a conquering act.

And when Antony died
she tricked her captors and killed herself—
an asp smuggled in a basket of figs.

Synesius to Hypatia, 3

> *I am in such evil fortune that I need a hydroscope. See that one is cast in brass for me and put together.*
>
> —written 402 CE

Hydroscopes measure the specific gravity of liquids.

No one knows why Synesius needed the hydroscope
or what he would do with it—whether to measure sugar in grape
juice, alcohol in wine or beer, creaminess in milk.

Synesius knew Hypatia would make the best one—

history's first mention of a device to weigh fluids.

Hypatia, perhaps inventor of the hydroscope,
her genius, calibrated by Synesius,
recorded in water.

Hypatia had uncommon force of character and ethical fortitude
and taught sophrosyne and dikaiosyne by example.
She practiced asceticism, chastity, restraint, and decency all her life.

Hypatia examined the good life,
left death to fate. Her murder completed historical
symmetry in Cleopatra's Caesareum.

Sometimes it's better
to be dead than alive and Cleopatra
knowing it was one of those times—
arranged her own death.

Hypatia's ethical fortitude meant she lived with hope,
self-control, and justice until her murder ushered

Alexandria into Christianity's shame, her city
no longer cosmopolitan haven for
Christians, Jews, and polytheists.

> *Some of those who wear the white and dark mantle have maintained that*
> *I am faithless to philosophy, apparently because I profess grace and*
> *harmony of style, and because I venture to say something concerning*
> *Homer and concerning the figures of the rhetoricians. In the eyes of such*
> *persons one must hate literature in order to be a philosopher and must*
> *occupy himself with divine matters only.*
> —probably written 402-403 CE

Synesius loved to hunt, defended the helpless, while his estate crumbled—

> his neighbours must have thought him an unlikely philosopher,
> at the time he sent *Dion*, his autobiography, to Hypatia

which also included mention of hatred for literature as requisite for a
philosopher.

Synesius is confident Hypatia would agree with him—

poetry and philosophy

are sisters.

The name Hypatia still represents
a thinking woman, brilliant in mathematics and sciences.

The puzzle of woman's pleasure,
riddle of her,

search for the feminine divine
in a rumour's answer upon her body.

Hypatia knew rumour's threat
to Christians and Jews:

> pleasure and divine,
> one vastly feminine cosmos.

> Babe in the womb,
> carbon in limestone,

> lightning storms here and on Jupiter
> and Venus, Earth's hotter sister.

> Sandstorms on Mars,
> Egyptian spring.

> Fulfillment what the eye sees
> and some of what it doesn't.

Synesius to Hypatia, 5

I account you as the only good thing that remains inviolate, along with
virtue. You always have power, and long may you have it and make
good use of that power. I recommend to your care Nicaeus and Philolaus.
— written 413 CE, his fourth last letter

Iniquity comes to Synesius. Before he knows his children will die
      Libyan nomads attack his home on the Cyrenaica terraces
leaving it the most derelict since his bishopric commenced.

Synesius recommends the young men, Nicaeus and Philolaus, as disciples
      to Hypatia and her power, not aware life in Alexandria is changing
and virtue's power, especially Hypatia's, will be punished more than ever.

The only good thing in his life violated, and he has no idea
      Hypatia is swimming dangerous waters. Only her name
testifies to her wise use of power.

Hypatia left her house alone, by chariot,
on the day of her death as was her custom.

Hypatia's connections to a great man her mistake.

Hypatia's lack of connection to a great man her mistake.

Of this we can be certain: her mistakes were one
and many, including being not a part of Neoplatonic theurgy,
her own rituals. All her own fault:
her birth, her low-class gender
as well as her aristocracy.

We can be assured
she deserved
what she got.

According to the Roman conquerors, her genius was in her non-existent
scrotum. Therefore, she had no genius and was not a great figure.

She could not have genius because she did not have
testicles to link her to land on which she lived in Egypt
She had no land in Rome, only in the Roman Empire,
if she had any at all, we don't know, and therefore
most definitely could not have had genius.

Colonials and women cannot have genius. Her aristocratic status was no help to her in the matter. Greeks thought Roman civilization brutal and stupid. No one could stop Romans from being that.

Synesius to Hypatia, 6

I have long been reproaching you that I am not deemed of a letter,
but now I know that I am despised by you all for no wrongdoing
on my part, but because I am unfortunate....
                           —written 413 CE, his second last letter

This is measure of his grief. Synesius believes Hypatia knew sorrow,
and she knew how to console—what Synesius craves.

Marauders stole Hypatia's letters we tell ourselves,
and Synesius remains desolate,
through history, his half:
Hypatia's unrecorded biography.

Hypatia was a benign Neoplatonist—
nothing out of the ordinary there.

Burnt white beach, fireflies
in star light, winking
sails upon aquamarine—

> since Alexander founded his town
> armaments have ruined fishing and
> philosophers have improved upon Plato
> adding soul to his hypotheses
> godlessly.

Synesius to Hypatia, 7

> *I am dictating to you from my bed, but may you receive it in good*
> *health, mother, sister, teacher and withal benefactress... May I cease*
> *to live, or cease to think of the tombs of my sons!*
> —written 413 CE, his last letter

Synesius dies within months of this letter—
       presumably thinking of the tombs of his sons.
He wishes Hypatia, and everyone who loves her as he does,
happiness. Synesius gives up hope of seeing her again
or hearing her voice. We join him, we who never will.

His pain from Hypatia's absence
greater than ours. Ours not inconsiderable.

We leave heartbroken Synesius here.

Hypatia dies in 415, two years later.

Synesius's sorrows flood time's underground river
it flows with grief, there is no consolation
in its alluvial sand, sun, and tall grasses

      history still misses her authority.

Hypatia, like Plato, probably thought democracy mob rule.
*Philosopher-teachers at the Serapeum were also priests of the Hellenic
religion who worshipped the baboon-headed god, Thoth, and taught the
lower classes. Hypatia had no truck with them.*

Swim-around search for Hypatia:
like salmon in the Columbia River of the twenty-first century—

women and genus *Oncorhynchus* insignificant or else they would be in the river
in the first place. Or could never be removed
without trace in riparian minerals.

Hypatia's ideas drown in water.

Her mother's shredded name and spent life
written in milk, parsed waves, food for fish;
this fluid condition excludes women from philosophy.

SYNESIUS TO HYPATIA, 8

I have lost my children, my friends, and the goodwill of everyone.
The greatest loss of all, however, is the absence of your divine spirit.
—written 413 CE, his second last to her, to anyone

Synesius did not give up his wife
when he became bishop; he never once in his writing
gives us her name.

She was like the weather, the air he breathed, nameless.

Not unusual but nevertheless a disappointment. He seems like such a
nice guy. History is merciless that way.

Synesius had three sons by this good Christian he married in Alexandria,
likely in the presence of Hypatia, whom he also lost, as have we, and
her mother's name with her. The wife of Synesius also
in that Aeolian purse where women's names
are snatched from history.

Hypatia, probably with Orestes, supported the Jews
of Alexandria. And this seems to have caused part of Cyril's jealousy.

Hypatia appeared to be motherless—her mother's anonymity
built-in invisibility for women—

> her mother may have
> taught her to be, to keep
> her self.

Hypatia was both perfect *other*
and imperfect one unpolluted by semen.

Hypatia forever non-adult—
did not give birth to flesh, man's property.

In truth, she had more influence
than most men.

Hypatia entertained Idea and
reined in stars with her astrolabe.

Forever attractive and taunted since—even dead she's not safe
from some man's idea of romance i.e. attack.

I swim up close, touch her shoulder
and see her turn to face me,
this different time in fluidity:
       she is dead, dead, dead.
       I am alive and
       by some lucky accident

want to ask her how a woman
can swim *materia*, slimy weeds
below, snakes coming
from the river bottom;
how it is that women, subject
to procreativity, harbour
the race our bodies terrify.

Things which are equal to the same thing are also equal to one another.

Hypatia probably considered Cyril, Patriarch of Alexandria,
and Synesius, reluctant bishop of Cyrene, as equals;
celibate priests equal to one another.

She menstruated and wore the white tribon of a scholar,
committed to her profession and class.

Hypatia in a double bind: of the class but not in the class.

Menstruation *equals* sign of dedication to philosophy and science.
Menstruation *equals* not pregnant or lactating to progress the class.
Suckling babies would also make her unclean.

Ergo, unclean equals menstruation.

Famous story about Hypatia, as reliable as the one about her death,
and often passed over. About the young man, hopelessly in love with
Hypatia.
She rubs his nose in her bloody sanitary napkin:
This is what you are in love with!
she tells the young pup.

What we cannot speak about we must pass over in silence,
said Ludwig, centuries later.

Double Bind

If Hypatia complied with men who lusted after her she'd have
been unclean for other reasons. She knew that things equal to
the same things are equal to one another. Euclid must have
been a deep comfort to her.

Therefore, etc.,
QED.
(.)(.)

A reliable way to understand Hypatia and her importance to her world
and ours is to look at her students and followers. Her popularity
among young people made her something like a Socrates of Africa,
many have noted. Her punishment by murder was much less
respectful than the death by hemlock of Plato's Socrates, whose
existence is arguable. Hypatia existed.

Murderous, the political correctness of Alexandria in the year 415.

Either you were for or against Christians—

> Hypatia was neither for, nor
> against them. Thoughtfulness and wisdom—

her undoing:
she had to be killed,

dismembered with oyster shells/broken roof tiles,
her quivering flesh fed to the fire,

precedent set.

Christendom's methodology for dealing
with troublesome women by fire
may have begun then.

But it's probably older than that.

Satan, a Christian god, like the other ones,
Father, Son, and the Holy Ghost who were making their first appearance
as one incredible god, seems to be asserting himself.

The method is this:
    take Satan's stance;
    beat Satan at his game,
    take knowledge from the tree of good and evil
    write hell
    x here.

Euclid's UnCommon Notions—Number Two

If equals be added to equals, the wholes are equals.

The real comes out
in the wash, the proof's
in the pudding,

QED or *that which has to be done.*

Look away dear girls—

       since before Eve and the serpent

       if the child born in sorrow

       is a girl, then not equal

       and if a boy, equal.

Euclid, Euclid, knows not.

Therefore, etc.,
QED.
(.)(.)

To Hypatia mathematics and astronomy were stepping stones
to the philosophy of being, Ontology. She regarded astronomy as the
highest knowledge.

Goddesses made in the image of mortal women
happen only in the heavens

a nowhere of no-thought:

they represent us, in opposition
they are the upper, we mortals the lower. Goddesses are
symbols of failure, deal with machinations of unfairness,
while women deal with facts.

       Utopia: a daughter powered by her mother's milk
       and language, blood's connection made visible,
       a new dyad.

EUCLID'S UNCOMMON NOTIONS—NUMBER THREE

If equals are subtracted from equals, then the remainders are equal.

Subtract Hypatia from her class of equals—
        we who wake Hypatia ponder human magnitudes
        Euclid hadn't contemplated. He was blind
to other uses of his notions.
        Aristocracy *minus* Hypatia *equals* Aristocracy *minus* Orestes
        Aristocracy *minus* Orestes *equals* Aristocracy *minus* Hypatia
But wait. She was peerless—Hypatia had no equal.
          After all, Greek civilization fell with her.
          No other women with Hypatia at Orestes' house
          or at Cyril's house. She had no peers, male or female,
          in her class. And none in any other class.
Time holds her, equal to air, a river we breathe.

        a) History *minus* Hypatia *equals* History *minus* Orestes
        QED etc. Zero game.
          No friction for Cyril, no murder of Hypatia,
          nothing for Christianity to overcome in Alexandria.
          Peter the Reader not famous
          for casting the first stone.
        b) History *minus* Orestes *equals* History *minus* Hypatia
        QED etc.
          Same as before but different.
          Hypatia might not have angered Cyril. Orestes
          would not have angered Cyril. (Someone else
          would have.)
          Orestes might have died peacefully in Alexandria.
        c) History *minus* Cyril *equals* History *minus* Orestes
        QED etc.
          History would have been totally different with
          equally unknown results.   QED etc.

d) History *minus* Hypatia *equals* History *minus* Cyril
QED etc.

> No Hypatia, no Cyril *equals* peace.
> Rome might not have fallen, nor Alexandria.
> Instead Orestes might have ruled happily,
> died in his Alexandrian bed, praised for
> accomplishment
> as prefect of Alexandria, ergo, Orestes
> not disappeared from history.

Subtracting Hypatia impossible, even if she is invisible, in
terms of magnitude.
Magnitudes of equal presence are not really equal it appears.
Equal magnitude subtracted from equal magnitude *equals*
more inequality in human classes of beings.
Euclid two.
History one.
But—

Therefore, etc.,

QED.

(.)(.)

Damascius writes, "the whole city doted on her and worshipped her."
Hypatia was showered with civic honours. Cyril was disliked from the beginning. He had the support of the clergy, the monks, some of the elite, and the pollon plethos *who had already destroyed Jewish dwellings.*

Feminine imagination in cells, dream, and exultation,
great fluidity loves and parses civilization—
                                    an underground river

            girls need

                                                women

            top-side vision

                                    Hypatia-like

            star-knowledge

                                    earth's mother

                            star-dust

carbon

                                        fallen

        from

                        infinite

                            space

EUCLID'S UNCOMMON NOTIONS—NUMBER FOUR

Things that coincide with one another equal one another.

Hypatia's brilliance will equal another woman's brilliance
who also had a father determined to make
a perfect person of his child.

Jean-Jacques' son, Émile Rousseau? *Mais non!*
Jean-Jacques intended to raise a perfect specimen of man.

Euclid's notion only works if something can be moved
in the way of superposition. Place Émile's position transparently
over Hypatia's and discrepancies appear.

Émile needed a girl, Sophie, who grew to be the ideal woman,
who corresponds with Émile, in temporal, and spatial terms.
They marry.

> *In what they have in common, they*
> *are equal. Where they differ, they are*
> *not comparable. A perfect woman and*
> *perfect man ought not to resemble each*
> *other in mind any more than in looks,*
> *and perfection is not susceptible of*
> *more or less.*
>
> from *Émile; or, On Education,*
> by Jean-Jacques 1762

Hypatia and Émile coincide in a patriarchal, genealogical way.
Superposition not possible, only ideal correspondence.
Sophie, that ideal woman, was unfaithful to Émile

in that she was raped by another
man and Sophie's rape
offended Émile and his family, their class,
with her uncleanliness.
Émile was forced to abandon her and his children.

Here we do have two things that coincide—
Hypatia and Sophie coincide
that double-bind kind of coincidence.
Therefore, etc.,
QED.
(.)(.)

"Nothing in Excess" and "Know Thyself,"

most famous adages at the Oracle of Delphi, were
taken seriously by Hypatia, who lived as a cultural Greek
in cosmopolitan Alexandria.

A wedding body of white,
shiny, plastic grocery bags

caught in a chain-link fence,
suspends prairie wind, abrading its gloss,

tearing spaghetti-like cells
from each other, impossible
decomposition.

It's not the dress but the body
for the wedding, walks
down the aisle,

death and rebirth
hover in tulle.

What a modern bride
can learn from Hypatia's life

what history and plastic carrier bag
have in common, how
we bring forth to mother.

The whole is greater than the part.

Much depends upon magnitude.

If Alexandria is the whole and the "greater than" of Hypatia,
if magnitude of Hypatia is zero,
then there is no remainder.

> Only reminder—
absence of her work which points to
a magnitude of zero.

What remains:
reports of her beauty and power.

Therefore, etc.,
QED.
(.)(.)

Hypatia's students had great affection for each other
and experienced many marvelous things, which they kept secret
to protect the knowledge and themselves.

The river of consciousness flows under stars
in blueblack night, a clitoris of time, circumscribed,
                              bobs among identities, declaring lineage,

girls and women.

At Hypatia's wake—
        rosy dawn rises perfectly
        catholic as feminine orgasm,
        engorging every member.

Stars shine after sunrise, Hypatia reminds us

even though we do not see stars, day robs sight,
and lights up Pythagoras's planets of divine vengeance,
to govern reincarnation.

        The river we're in
flows around us, begs for feminine genealogy
        as it swells and scours rock in a rite of cells,
remembers the girl's lesson—
invisibility.

René's Vicious Circle

::

René thinks

therefore he is

        floats viciously.

Hypatia thinks

therefore she isn't

        drowns miserably.

::

If Hypatia were the sea she would be
geometry, curved lines, no subject,

object of use, means of transport.
If Hypatia were the sea, she would be immense,

no thought could draw a line to erase her
and time would drown, its river swallowed

in estuary. If Hypatia were the sea, the sea would be dead
its use as transport and food and garbage disposal

fulfilled. If the sea were dead
Hypatia would still be dead

just as René thought
and therefore was.

More rumours spread among Cyril's followers that Hypatia was a witch,
practicing magic—devoted at all times to astrolabes, and instruments
of music; that she satanically cast spells on people, even Cyril who
was no longer going to church. (Now there's a double bind for you: the
bishop no longer attends church but murders another who never did—
ostensibly for not being a churchgoer.)

The divine above

        or beneath

hurts, asks why do we burn

skin's other side of history, the feminine;

silence redolent with damaged cells and atoms,

too much blood, shed of its beauty.

The chaos of Hypatia's wake enjoys

eternity's pleasure,

black space lit with millions of stars

cosmic beaches stretch below—

our ability to imagine symbol

creates divinity.

Hegel's Vicious Circle

In Georg Wilhelm Friedrich's version, Antigone/female, in
    Sophocles' play
is both unconscious and guilty. Biology determined her passivity
and duty to preserve family.

Hegel, who used his last name as first, wrote that Antigone's
    subversive activity
in burying her brother Polynices, enemy of state, was a crime against
    Creon's edict
and Antigone thereby entered political life illegitimately.

Creon is king and cannot be wrong.

::

> We in Hypatia's wake may question symbolic order
> in mythology and tragedy
>
> because they install themselves in our imagination
> and become law.
>
> Antigone is young, true, not anarchist
> or suicidal, not unconcerned with governing
>
> and believes in justice.
>
> Many say women are not in government
> because they do not wish to govern.

Antigone governs as far as
she is permitted before she must kill

herself after burying her brother.
Hegel needs synthesis. Either way,

Antigone must go.

Hypatia taught students from everywhere in the known world
and everywhere on the religious spectrum.

Biographies and Westerns, the same,
no girls—
only sluts
or saints.

> A double bind has genius in it.
> To tie up a woman
> in perennial efficiency—
> history goes forward
> and backward.

Take Hypatia—

she was young and pretty
and probably asking for it

She was old and powerful
and asking for it.

Either way, she deserved
everything she got,

preserving her almost non-place in history.
Drama involving a woman most notable

when she dies, preferably violently,
and better yet, young, and nubile.

HEGEL'S VICIOUS CIRCLE, AS PERTAINS TO HYPATIA
a

Woman is a woman and therefore
incapable of governing
because she is a woman.

Georg Wilhelm Friedrich's Antigone makes clear Hypatia's
mistake—
Hypatia had no religion so she could not bury
her dead brother for religious reasons.

She did not have a brother
and he did not die.

Hypatia's mistake was to live to be old
without a husband to baby or a brother to bury,
or an uncle to disobey.

Hypatia lived beyond these, dared to be
philosopher, death knell to her pleasure, divinity.

Hypatia, an old woman, rejected freedom to kill herself,
her life not a tragedy while alive, she had influence
and lived to the last moment of her murder.

Hypatia was a "genuine guide in the mysteries of philosophy"
(gneisa kathegemon ton philosophias orgion)—Maria Dzielska

In the historic present of Hypatia's wake
her chariot not yet ready, she
lives a few hours longer.

Last time to see Hypatia, as she is,
last time she smiles at a student, nods to a free man,
smoothes the robe caught in her sandal.

Hypatia ordained by her mother on an ordinary day—
her murder defines/aligns women who think.

HEGEL'S VICIOUS CIRCLE, AS PERTAINS TO HYPATIA
b

Her birth makes Hypatia the perfect philosopher now:
                    not only no longer born
                    but dead.

                    If she thinks, it's un-thought.

                    Her severed flesh
                    flame in air
                    ashes return
                    to her stars.

                    Drowned idea is still idea
                    and may be found in what drowned it.
::

Hypatia's other mistake, a Freudian one, was to be not-mother.
As a mother she may have fulfilled expectations of familiar forgettability,

how she might have made life for women more just. We only know
her death and disappearance from history's full accounting.

The underside of good orderly government that killed Hypatia
is the same domestic violence that kills today,

steals mothers and grandmothers, sisters and aunts, robs
feminine power from girls who are nature-in-training, their minds

accessories worn to prettify consciousness as mother or not. If not
mother then nothing, the other woman. Them's her choices.

Hypatia taught in a closed circle. **Her students**
came to her house daily and followed a secret schedule.
Hypatia, a Platonic scholar, taught the history of
philosophy, and followed in Plotinus's Neoplatonism.

Something in Hypatia leapt to the dust
and profusion of ethers and storms

to joy of knowing the stars,
superstition about planets swept aside.

Hypatia may have known Earth is a planet too
in harmony with other geometries—

bodies fall down, not up, and spheres play
in harmony, Earth a province of the cosmos.

Fallible order includes famines
in every time.

Nothing changes Hypatia's wake.
The moon passively white and cratered, revolves

force behind the fall,
orbits equal.

Isaac's genius discovery in his miracle year of 1666
rested upon Hypatia's work: *Euclid's Elements of Geometry.*

Hypatia fell into history's abyss.
Isaac's posterity good, standing

on a giant or two. We swim the rivers
materia and consciousness

their plait of time, delight upon awakening,
meeting again, ancient and current

we know but we don't know we know
                    Hypatia's presence

our blue jewel
lapis gravitas.

HEGEL'S VICIOUS CIRCLE, AS PERTAINS TO HYPATIA
c

::

When Hypatia's mother became weather

                              and light

Hypatia understood time's geometry

filled with nothing, empty of nothing.

Hypatia studied and navigated stars,

stability outside of time's plane.

Or so I imagine

Hypatia and her mother.

Knowledge of a mother's influence on a philosopher

as unknown as mothers are unknown.

Hypatia left her house by chariot the day she was killed
as she often did, en route to Alexandria's
lecture halls, when invited to speak.

Antonius, son of the woman Sosipatra of Pergamum, was an eminent
Neoplatonic philosopher
    who may have inducted her into Chaldean mysteries.
Antonius had a genealogic link to his mother.

No genealogy links Hypatia
to her mother, or any other.

                              Lunar maria, plural
                              seas on the moon,

                    basaltic plains, old volcanoes.
                              Hypatia may have

                              remarked upon this
                                          other
                              side of red,
                              beyond violet

                                  I am visible
                              in the middle.

Hypatia did not understand invisible—
she had no way to account for objects

in a darkened room. She believed her eyes emitted
rays to give sight. Nevertheless,

Hypatia comes with me
to the basement's night, heavy

as Venus atmosphere
feeling for the switch, eyes

in our fingers, Neoplatonically
being what we see.

Hypatia's String Theory

The varieties of science, rolled up
like thread on spools, infinitesimally small,
cloud spun into small and smaller dimensions

pull of moon and stars
equal to the distance from Earth's pull
(we're talking gravity here, not *gravitas*)

ends and depths of existence
are closer than we think
if we could only see

outside the slice of discovery. Our galaxy turns
inside out like an Egyptian pillowcase in Hypatia's house
feathery geometry falls, snow of particles,

hints for the dubious, along a membrane of doubt,
as time unwinds
and atoms unite, reunite, and break apart.

Girls fall into galaxies
gravity acts according to laws
a girl in late antiquity or modern Egypt

nearly always obeys—not only nature
but limits on thought relative to the moon's force,
thought's acceleration—smaller than the apple in her hand.

Seed, germ, cell,
charm—*think therefore I am.*
Seeds in the girl/fruit of the womb/

thought in the man: we are
alike, light instant.
Time dilates at high speed,

specularization of mother
nature, René and I/eye,
science slips by.

Isaac's second law of motion, F=ma
equivalent to the girl's attraction to earth, as she
falls, gravitationally—*to be continued*

Hypatia was an aristocrat and so were her students.

They never strayed from their class to help lower classes. They saw other philosophers, wearing white mantles, as lower-class, mere sophists, and the monks, wearing black mantles, as basket-weaving barbarians. This attitude was perhaps a source of hostility toward her.

Space around her body breathed, morning star a guide,

particularities mathematically true to navigations behind

skin's veil. All she needed to know, as she taught

comfort in the elegance of integers, uncovered

mystery in sky and heart. Perhaps her students

adored her for her inclusive love of earth.

No duality too large to unify:

proof's burden never too difficult.

Perhaps Hypatia also trusted death's friendly justice.

not equal to the speed of light, longevity
an old woman and elegant geometry.
Hypatia's astrolabe, star tracker, predicts

heavenly bodies' trace of song's weight
jumpy jive and the spheres' music
on a string.

Hypatia knew dualities, Platonic and scientific.
She understood mathematics unites, joins, extends,
draws, and intersects any two points by a straight line.

A cone intersects the plane, winds its radius,
equations shift as time piled upon silence in her body.

She understood the need for gods although she pondered
their passing, knew their every guise.

Hypatia was about sixty years old

> *when she was murdered. This is the kicker: she was beautiful*
> *but not young, an old woman with great intellectual power and*
> *empire-wide influence. Much of what has been written assumed*
> *she was young and asking for it by being too beautiful.*

1
(.)(.)

Underground river retreats to air,

hosts Hypatia's wake—

found in the riverbed, in her millions,

too dead to be alive, too alive to be dead

shades,

ghost presence

we

the great fluidity.

2
(.)(.)

Hypatia gave no man
her flesh as property: her slit, her clit,
    neck of her womb, her breasts, her belly,
her body for herself, its own pleasure.

        Her tearing apart occurred at death,
        not in giving life.

This appeared to be her greatest sin—not to mention
wise tongue in her head, compassion in her breast.

        These were deadly, not hers to give,
          parabalani, the murderous
          monks reasoned, as they
          acted for the bishop to take
          down
          this woman.

By law, her parts belonged to men, to do with as they wished.

They did.

Hypatia's line from her mother strangled,
history's neglect.

3
(.)(.)

A woman's   hole   in society

                    woman contains *man*

                    whole contains *hole*.

Distortion, a dirty touch, inevitable when words contain

                    other words.

Hypatia, a hole in the plywords of history and knowledge—

            to think for oneself a hole in the vicious circle—

her form her own, her pleasure possible

without language, words all over her body

owned by her own self. Hypatia was whole and without.

History has a hole   named Hypatia.

4
(.)(.)

Hypatia in the great fluidity—

I step into this river twice, swim with
torn sleeve, scarlet and rust,
azure trinkets on thought's pocket

        ripped from thought's bodice
        float in our wake
        as I follow her.

Bobcat down the ridge: I see him from my window
either his gamble in spring's hunt or my acuity
to see the cat's stealth and perkiness.

Our eachness at Hypatia's wake:

        thought rushing through.

        Pansies erupt from snow,

        cedar, and bobcat

        their proper size and shape

        blur horizon.

5
(.)(.)

Dawn rinses the coast
and pinks our skyline
in the historic present of
Hypatia's wake

Maybe an elephant in Hypatia's dream
the night before
screams in terror
before a mob:

> monks from the mountains
> form a deadly collective—
> the horizon red.

6
(.)(.)

Torn vestments and wisdom litter
a mountain of thinking about Hypatia—
                        navigated stars,
                        underground river,

swells wake upon ears—

language lost, signs buried, maps ript,
scattered in brain's runnels

separated and joined
eternally now.

Hypatia thought her own way, I remind myself.

Scruples fall in spring's week-long tenure.

Her thinking tissue like mine, mother
mirror for me, although she was never a mother

and I have been: issue of my body and mind
incorporated in three persons who remember baths

and Nivea Creme, the blue jar
icon of love's silky texture.

The Flesh of Invisibility

A man minus the possibility of representing
oneself as a man = a normal woman.
Luce Irigaray

If you are a woman archives hold perpetual ironies.
Because the gaps and silences are where you find yourself.
Susan Howe

If we are single, they say we couldn't catch a man,
if we are married, they say we're neglecting him,
if we are divorced, that we couldn't keep him,
if we are widowed, they say we killed him.
Kathleen Brown, USA gubernatorial candidate

When my children acquired paper routes, our household's free subscription caused me to become a desultory reader of the newspaper. Turns out, the news was riddled with typos and grammatical errors. And I began to check headlines to see what was worth the price of exasperation. The obituaries attracted me because real stories are told there, and with sincerity. When cause of death wasn't mentioned, I found myself burning with curiosity at the omission of an important aspect of plot. And in what became an after-supper, extra-cup-of-tea ritual I did the crossword puzzles too.

During the tenure of our subscription, I made an informal and loose survey of human subjects of photos, mostly men, in the newspaper. My study had not a shred of science and I didn't write anything down. Women in the newspaper were predominantly young and attractive, scantily clothed or injured in car accidents, stabbed, carried away on stretchers, etc. I mentioned this observation to friends who started to read the paper as critically and concurred with my findings. I assume it was not official editorial policy but only a reflection of reality, according to someone. I came to the informal conclusion that newsworthy women were necessarily young and sexy or else injured and/or dead, retooling an aphorism, *the only good woman is a dead one*. I mentioned this a few times too often, irritating my kids and their friends who were probably glad their mothers didn't say things like that. *Curiosity killed the cat* I reminded myself, curious since birth and annoying people ever since. Coincidentally, I became interested at that time in Hypatia of Alexandria, fifth-century philosopher, mathematician, and astronomer whom history treated the same as the newspaper did the young women in our city of 250,000 souls. I continued my informal study of our society's interest in injured/injuring female subjects until the kids grew out of paper routes. The flesh of invisibility is my term for the absence of women in aspects of society, culture, and history.

The 'flesh' in what I call the *flesh of invisibility* is borrowed from Maurice Merleau-Ponty, the French phenomenologist (1908-1961), and his philosophical use of *la chair* (flesh) in the working notes for *The Visible and the Invisible*, published posthumously. Flesh, for Merleau-Ponty, refers both to the invisible aspects of perception and the participation in being since the beginning of time.

A band of monks murdered Hypatia of Alexandria, in 415 CE. Hypatia's father was Theon of Alexander (335-405), Greek scholar and mathematician, and that fact is the first and main reason we know of her. We know nothing of her mother, who must have done an excellent job. That we know who murdered her is the second reason we know of Hypatia. Her death gave victory to Christianity, and we know that victors write history. Political jealousies between Orestes, the prefect of Roman Alexandria, and Cyril, Bishop of Alexandria, seem to be the reason for her murder.

The difference between invisibility and imperceptibility exists although what we don't perceive may as well be invisible, as attested by Hollywood's lack of roles for women. We may not perceive, in a conscious manner, that we breathe air: we live without noticing that oxygen comes to us through our breathing. When we swam as fish in our mother's wombs, we didn't need oxygen, but the second we encountered air we began to breathe. We take breathing for granted, until oxygen disappears and then it's too late. But that doesn't mean that oxygen doesn't have the most central importance to life.

We notice the lack of oxygen, or hypoxia, in our bodies by our fatigue, headaches, dizziness, shortness of breath, a bluish tone in the nail beds of our fingers and toes and around the mouth, before loss of consciousness, and then death, arrive. When anoxia, or complete deprivation of oxygen occurs, the organism dies. The state of women in history and culture persists like a permanent case of low-grade hypoxia.

We take culture for granted, as we do the act of breathing. As social creatures, we breathe culture passed on, generation-to-generation, and rarely question it. We perceive aspects of our culture when we suddenly notice things as I did photos in the newspaper. When we notice that large groups, such as women, who are more than half the world's population, seem expendable, then we question the culture we live in.

Flesh of invisibility, it appears, is a condition brought about by history and culture, as involuntary as breathing. It is the lack of perception of a lack of perception. Women, poor people, enslaved persons of all sorts, and many children live in this state. The fact of the flesh of invisibility in the past helps us to understand it in the present, just as Hypatia's life in the margins helps me understand history. The fact that we know nothing of Hypatia's mother is a sign of what Luce Irigaray, French contemporary theorist, alludes to when she writes: "A man minus the possibility of representing oneself as a man = a normal woman." History makes it seem that Hypatia lived in a state of *déréliction*, i.e., a state of being abandoned by her mother. Hypatia's mother was unable to present herself as a man, whereas Hypatia almost did. As a chaste virgin she was free of men.

—And that's the rub: women's history is invisible for the most part and yet it exists. If women do not partake in the history of the world it is because we do not partake of institutions and culture as full beings. If we have no history, it's because we are not visible beings. If we are not visible, it's often because we lack rights. Rights can't be granted to invisible entities. If we are not visible it's not because we are not flesh of the world. We partake of invisibility involuntarily.

If you are a woman, the flesh of invisibility is somewhat automatic. Hypatia has suffered invisibility retroactively but in her lifetime she was eminently visible, and that appears to be the cause of her murder. Men, women, and children suffer from the loss of what is stolen by the flesh of invisibility; it is like an amputated limb to the flesh of the world when parts of humanity are not allowed to act. If we look closely, we women will find those ironic places, gaps, in the archives and history books where we exist just as we know Hypatia's mother must have existed although her name has never been recorded. Hypatia lived and the flesh of her invisibility has not stolen her from us forever. We can claim her and wake her loss as we are awakened to her. When we give Hypatia back to the flesh of the world, we claim visibility.

And perhaps we need to remember that visibility is dangerous and proceed under the sign of Hypatia, invoking her protection.

(.)(.)

ACKNOWLEDGEMENTS

Some of the poems, or earlier versions, appeared in the following anthologies and periodicals:

>Tsiang, Sarah Yi-Mei, editor. *Desperately Seeking Susans.* Oolichan Books, 2013.

>Fertig, Mona and Harold Rhenisch, editors. *RockSalt, an Anthology of Contemporary BC Poetry.* Mother Tongue Publishing, 2008.

>*CV 2,* vol. 35, no. 1, Summer 2012.

Thanks to Luciana Ricciutelli, to Renée Knapp, Ashley Rayner, and the team at Inanna Publications who continue Luciana's legacy. Gratitude to Chelene Knight for editorial clarity, Val Fullard for thoughtful cover design, and Linda Besner for impeccable care with language.

Grateful acknowledgement is made to the British Columbia Arts Council for assistance in the form of a grant.

Thanks also to Maria Dzielska for *Hypatia of Alexandria* (Harvard University Press, 1995) and her reliable scholarship.

Many thanks for support and encouragement to Eileen Delehanty Pearkes, Jana Danniels, Bobbie Ogletree, Jane Byers, and Linda Crosfield. Remembering Anne Szumigalski, with gratitude, for conversations about Hypatia in Anne's kitchen.

Lasting love and gratitude to Gord Andrews who has adventured in life with me and to whom this book is dedicated.

Credit: Jeremy Addington

Susan Andrews Grace lives in Nelson, British Columbia where she maintains a visual art practice and teaches at Oxygen Art Centre.